Most Popular
African Safari Animals

Billy Grinslott & Kinsey Marie Books

ISBN - 9781965098295

Elephant Shrews have long, legs for their size. They move in a hopping motion like rabbits. Being one of the fastest small rodents, the elephant shrew can run at almost 20 miles per hour.

Elephant shrews use their long nose to search for food. They can smell in between rocks and other crevices. Elephant shrews can jump three feet into the air, giving them the nickname jumping shrew.

Rock Hyraxes are unique in that the iris slightly protrudes over the pupil of their eye. Rock hyraxes can climb on steep rock surfaces because of physical adaptations on their feet. Hyraxes have long hairs scattered over their bodies. Rock Hyraxes spend a lot of time sun-bathing. The rock hyrax spends about 95 percent of its time resting.

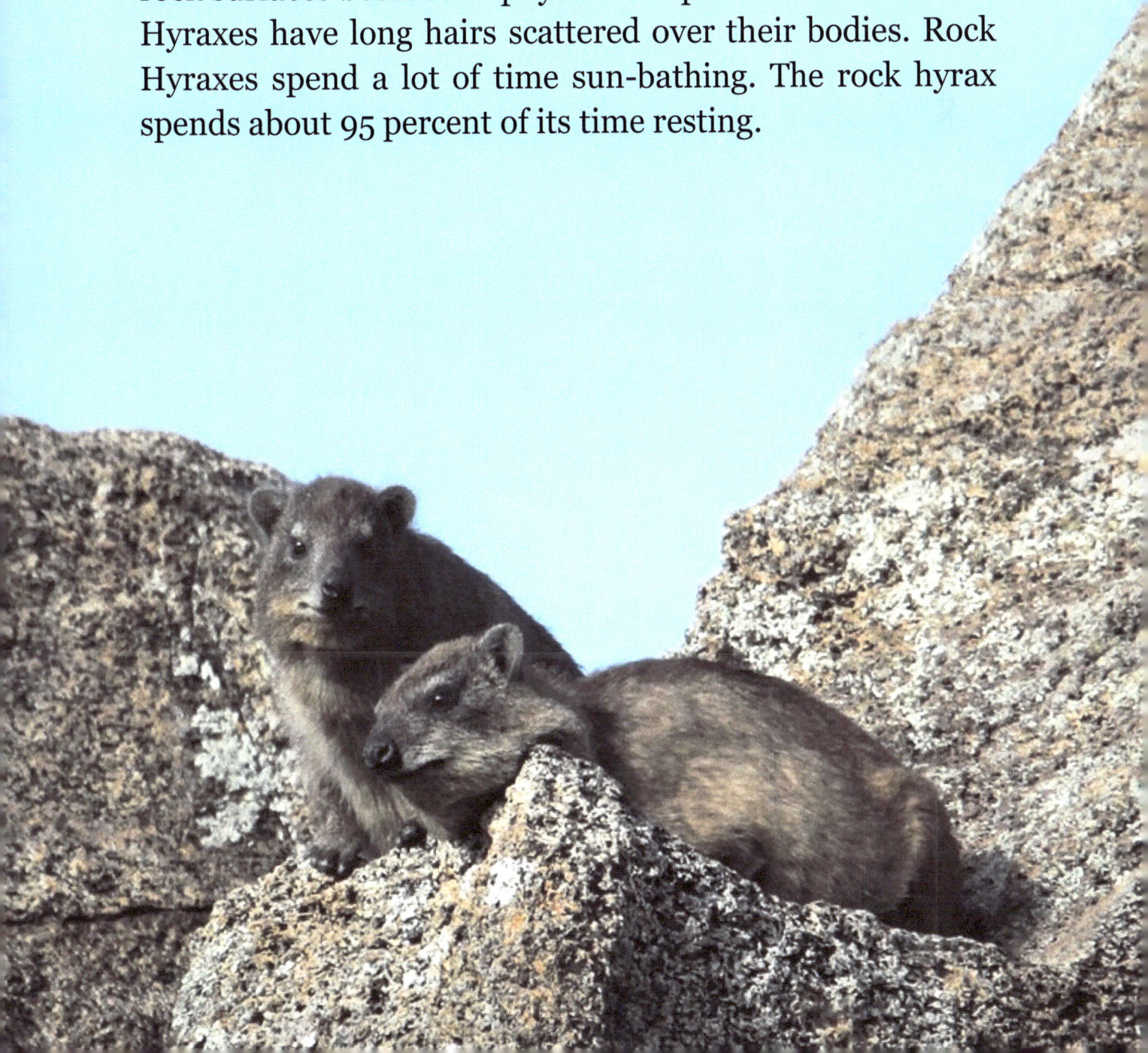

Meerkats are immune to some snake's venom as they belong to the mongoose family. Meercats can also eat scorpions because they are immune to their venom. Meerkats are smart and have problem solving capabilities. They can spot birds miles away. They have dark patches around their eyes to cut down glare from the sun and help them see far into the distance.

The big eyes of a bush baby allow it to see in very low light and darkness. Bush babies are adapted to nocturnal living. The cry of a bush baby sounds very similar to a crying human baby. They have large ears for great hearing and can jump long distances.

This is an Aardvark, also known as an ant eater. They love to eat ants and termites. They can eat up to 50 thousand ants and termites a day. They have sharp claws to dig with and a long nose to grab food out of holes or ant mounds. The name aardvark means ground pig, they look like small pigs with a long nose.

Porcupines have sharp quills on their backs to help protect them. A porcupine can have up to 30 thousand quills, they are sharp and will stick you if you touch them. Baby porcupines are born with soft, bendable quills that begin to harden within a few days after they are born. To communicate they make grunts and high-pitched noises. A group of porcupines is called a family.

This is a honey badger. They get their name because they like to eat sweet stuff like honey, but they will eat anything. They kind of look like skunks with their light colored back and tail. They have long claws to dig burrows to rest in. They will dig a whole anywhere. Honey badgers are very smart. One honey badger broke out of his cage by opening gates and creating stacks of rocks to get over walls. They can adapt to any situation.

Pangolin means roller. When a Pangolin is in danger, it will roll up into a ball and can be rolled around. They have a hard shell that also protects them. There are eight species of pangolin, and they are built like an armadillo. They have sharp front claws for digging.

Unlike other cranes, crowned cranes usually roost in trees. They can flock in large numbers, anywhere between 30 and 150. The grey crowned crane is the national bird of Uganda. The chicks are 'precocial' which means they can run as soon as they hatch. The grey crowned crane puts on a great display involving dancing, bowing, and jumping.

The ostrich has the longest legs and neck of any bird species. Ostriches can't fly even though they have wings. They run instead of flying. With their long legs they can run up to 45 miles per hour. Ostrich's legs are strong, and they can front kick other animals. Ostriches live in small flocks and check their eggs by sticking their head into the hole where their eggs are. Ostriches like water and enjoy taking baths.

The lesser flamingo is one of the smallest and the brightest of the flamingos. Lesser flamingos do not migrate, and they live in big colonies with sometimes more than 1 million birds. They are mostly active at night. They fly between water bodies in large, V-shaped formations when food sources have become depleted.

The Shoebill stork gets its name from its beak, which looks like a pair of old-style clog shoes. The shoebill stork looks like a prehistoric animal. Shoebill storks have a habit of shaking their heads back and forth and they chatter their beaks together as a type of communication.

No one is quite sure how the secretary bird got its name. Its scientific name means, the archer of snakes. They rarely fly and mostly feed on the ground. Secretary birds have one of the strongest and fastest kicks in the animal kingdom. It has a distinctive appearance, it has the body of an eagle, but the legs of a crane. The long legs make it look tall.

The African penguin has a black stripe and a pattern of unique black spots on its chest, as well as pink glands above its eyes that become pinker as the penguin gets hotter. African penguins are believed to be one of the first penguins to be discovered by humans. They can live in hot and cold temperatures.

Dugongs are more related to elephants than other marine mammals like whales and dolphins. They rarely communicate visually with each other, because they have poor eyesight. Instead, they use sounds and physical touch to communicate with each other. Because their diet consists of mainly seagrass, they are nicknamed sea cows. Dugongs sing to each other all the time, using chirps, whistles, barks and other sounds that echo through the water.

Monitor Lizards are cousins to the Komodo dragon. The Komodo dragon, famous for its large size and powerful bite, is a type of monitor lizard. Monitor Lizards are very smart and have a great sense of smell. They use the saliva on their long tongues to help smell stuff. They also use their tails like weapons, to swat things. While the monitor uses its venom to kill small prey, it has a mild effect on humans.

The leopard tortoise is one of the largest tortoises. It gets its name from the markings on its shell that resemble the large spotted cat, the leopard. Leopard tortoises can live for 75 years. They are the only tortoise that can raise their head up due to their shell design.

A crocodile's jaws can apply 5,000 pounds of pressure per square inch, the strongest bite of any animal in the world. Crocodiles can lose up to 4,000 teeth over a lifetime. Crocodiles are fast over short distances. Crocodiles are one of the only animals that are thought to have survived the asteroid that wiped out the dinosaur population. They are one of the oldest reptiles to live on earth.

There are both monkeys and Chimpanzees in Africa. They are skilled climbers and like hanging out in trees. There are 200 species of monkeys and chimps. They are smart and even use rocks and sticks as tools. The howler monkey makes the loudest noises. Monkeys and chimpanzees love to eat fruits and vegetables, like bananas. Grooming each other is a sign of affection and helps build strong relationships.

Vervet monkeys are small, gray-colored monkeys with black faces. Vervet monkeys are as comfortable on the ground as they are in trees. They are active in the daytime and sleep in trees at night. They are considered to be one of the most widespread monkeys in Africa. They spend several hours a day grooming each other's fur.

There are five species of baboons. Male baboons are two times larger than females. Baboons live in groups called troops. Baboons use 30 different sounds to communicate. Baboons can survive up to 30 years. Baboons will eat any type of food that is available.

Mandrills are the largest monkey species and one of the most colorful. They resemble baboons, but they are more closely related to mangabey monkeys. They look like baboons but have a few different markings.

Gorillas have hands and feet like humans including thumbs and big toes. Some gorillas have learned to use sign language to communicate with humans. Gorillas pound their chest as a type of communication. People share around 98% of our DNA with gorillas. They are one of the biggest, most powerful living primates. They have 16 different types of calls. Gorillas live in small groups called troops or bands. They live up to 35 years.

Fennec fox is the world's smallest fox. The average fennec fox is only about 8 inches tall and weighs up to 3 pounds. Fennec foxes have extraordinary hearing to locate underground animals. Their large ears help to dissipate excess body heat on hot days. The fennec fox appears to be the only carnivore in the Desert able to live without available water.

A male bat eared fox is called a dog, a female is called a vixen and a baby is called a kit. Bat eared foxes can use their large ears to hear things at long distances and can even hear insects crawling underground. Bat eared foxes live in pairs or small groups. They spend most of the day sleeping and come together at dusk for playtime, social grooming before foraging throughout the night.

Black or silver backed jackals are highly vocal. Fossil deposits have revealed that the black backed jackal is one of the oldest known dog species. Jackal pairs do everything together, including eating and sleeping. Jackals make a very wide range of interesting sounds including whines, growls, cackling laughs, yelps and deep throaty yells.

African wild dog packs have high levels of communication with each other. The African wild dog can run up to 44mph, the same as a greyhound. Wild dogs only have four toes per forefoot. In addition, a wild dog's large, round ears allow them to keep track of pack members over long distances through audio signals. They have great hearing.

These are hyenas. They are very smart animals. They are very family orientated and make great mothers and take very good care of their young ones. Hyenas make a laughing or giggling noise, that's how they communicate. They can live up to 20 years, the longest of any canines. They are very social animals and like talking to each other and living in groups.

Aardwolves are related to hyenas. Aardwolf means earth wolf in Afrikaans. Aardwolves have cheek teeth that are flattened pegs, used for eating insects. They eat mostly termites. They spend their days underground and come out at night. Aardwolves can raise their mane hair to appear bigger than what they are. They raise their mane hair to scare off intruders. They communicate largely through smell.

Look there's a warthog. They are vegetarians and like to dig for roots and bulbs. They also like to eat grasses, plants, berries, and bark. Warthogs also like to wallow in the water to cool off. Their tusks are large canine teeth. They don't have warts. They have large bones and cartilage on the side of their face and that's how they get their name. They can run fast and are very family orientated even becoming foster parents to others young ones.

Springboks are widely distributed throughout South Africa and is also the National Animal of South Africa. Both male and females have horns. They are highly social and move around in large herds. There are some Springbok that are totally black or totally white in color. Springboks are related gazelles, which are small antelopes.

Gerenuk Deer has a long narrow neck. The gerenuk eats standing on two legs. They stand erect on their hind legs, with their long necks extended, to browse on tall bushes. By using their front legs to pull down higher branches, they can reach leaves six to eight feet off the ground.

The dik-dik is a very small antelope. It only grows about 15 inches high. They only weigh about 13 pounds. Most dogs way more than a dik-dik does. When dik-diks feel they're in danger, they hide instead of fleeing from predators. When frightened or disturbed, they make a whistling sound through their nose that sounds like "zik-zik," and this is probably how they got their name.

The impala is one of the most common and most graceful of all Africa's antelopes. They can run at speeds faster than 60km/h. They can leap as far as 33 feet and as high as 10 feet. The female is similar to the male but does not have horns. The male's graceful lyre-shaped horns are about 40 to 90 centimeters long.

This is a Gazelle. They are very fast. They like to live in herds. Gazelles don't outrun other animals. They out maneuver them. They can twist and turn very quickly. Both males and females have horns. They love to eat grass and other plants. They can easily climb rocks. They like to hang out with zebras.

Harnessed Bushbuck is chestnut red in color with a pattern of white spots and stripes on its flanks. They can adapt to a variety of habitats, from dense forests to open savannas. The harnessed Bushbuck is a medium-sized antelope, widespread in sub-Saharan-Africa. Bushbucks are solitary animals, and mature males try to stay away from each other.

The eland is the slowest antelope. It can only run about 25 mph, but it can jump 10 feet from a standing start. When walking, tendons or joints in the eland's foreleg produce a sharp clicking sound. The common eland is better adapted than cattle to the African environment and is easily domesticated.

Nyala are one of Africa's most alert antelopes. They have exceptional hearing and smell, as well as great eyesight to sense danger. Male nyala can be recognized by their horns, dark grey coat and pale stripes on their sides. Females and young ones have reddish fur with lighter stripes. The nyala is mainly active early in the morning and late in the afternoon. They inhabit the dry savannas and dense woodlands.

The Oryx is a large member of the antelope family. They are very distinctive due to their pale fur, dark facial markings, and long straight horns. Their long horns protect them from other animals. Oryx can survive a long time without water. Oryx travel in herds, but don't like to encounter other animals. There are 4 types of Oryxes. Both male and female Oryx have horns.

The Kudu is one of the largest members of the antelope family. They produce one of the loudest sounds made by antelope in the form of a gruff bark like a dog. Kudus have long horns with spirals that help protect them from other animals. Kudus are highly alert and hard to approach. Only male Kudus have horns that continue to grow.

Wildebeests are the largest member of the antelope family. There are two species of wildebeest. The blue wildebeest got their name because their coat has a blue sheen. They can run up to 40 mph, which is pretty fast! Wildebeests migrate as many as one thousand miles each year. Wildebeest are Playful and intelligent. They also like taking naps.

The Cape Buffalo is the most common in Africa. Their horns are curved and designed to protect their head. Buffalos communicate with each other by making low pitched sounds. Mother buffalos only have baby's during the rainy season in Africa. Calves will stay with their mother for a year. Then they become part of the herd.

Okapis belong to the Giraffe family. But are related to the zebra. That's why they have partial zebra stripes. They can stand on their back feet to eat leaves off trees. That's how they got the nickname of TreeHugger. Wild Okapis only live in the regions of Congo jungle in Africa.

Zebras and are part of the horse family, but they live in the wild. Zebras have light fur and black stripes that help to camouflage them. Zebras love to eat plants and grass. Newborn foals, baby zebras can stand after 6 minutes. Baby zebras have brown stripes when they are born and as they mature, they turn black. A herd or group of zebras is called a dazzle.

The civet is a small mammal native to tropical regions of Africa. The civet is known for its slender body, long tail, and distinctive facial markings. Civets are often called civet cats but, they are not cats. They are more closely related to mongooses. Civets are nocturnal, meaning they come out at night. There are over 30 different species of civets. They are excellent climbers and spend most of their time in the trees.

Genets are catlike animals with a tail usually as long as their body .Genets have retractable claws adapted to climbing like house cats do. Genets can climb trees. However, they also spend much time on the ground and take shelter in rocky areas. They can squeeze their flexible bodies through any opening that is larger than their head. Adult genets are solitary, spending much of their time alone.

Caracal Cats. Their name means cat with black ears. They are often confused with lynxes. Caracals are excellent climbers. They have 20 separate muscles in their ears. They can leap 10 feet into the air. Caracals live in many areas but prefer areas that have both tree cover with open areas.

Servals have the largest ears of any cat. Servals can jump high. Servals communicate with each other by peeing on things. Servals can purr just like house cats do. They also like to climb and sleep in trees.

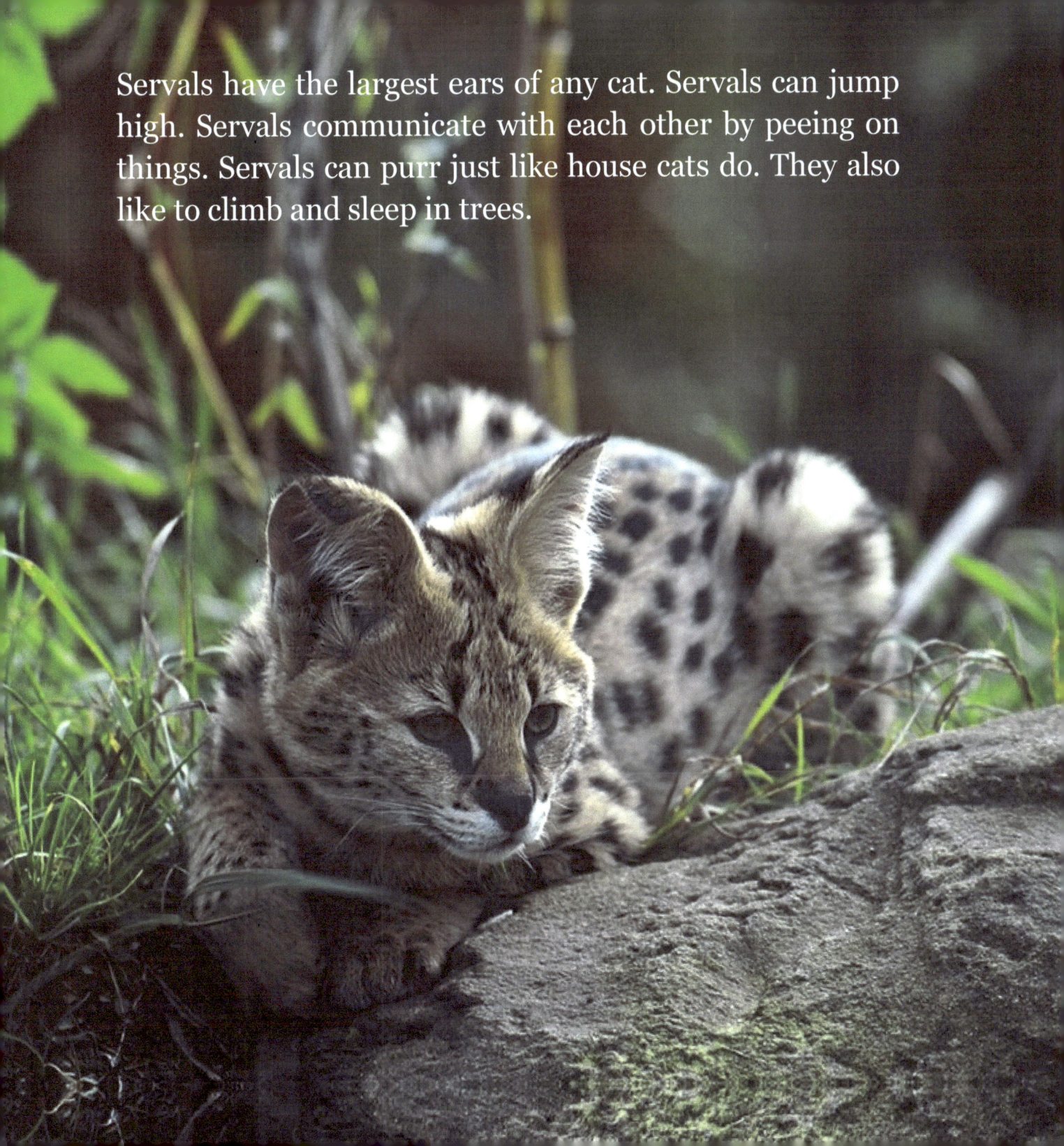

Leopards are sometimes confused with cheetahs because of their markings. The cheetah has black spots. The leopard has round markings called rosettes. Can you see the difference? Leopards are some of the strongest cats on earth. They can climb trees even while carrying another animal. They are very elusive and good at hiding. They can run up to 35 miles per hour. They can jump 20 feet in one bounce and jump 10 feet high. That's amazing.

Cheetahs are the fastest cats on the planet. They can run up to 60 miles per hour in just 3 seconds. That's fast. Cheetahs are built for speed. They have a flexible spine that allows them to stretch out on each stride. Cheetahs have black spots on their fur. Cheetahs don't roar like other big cats, they meow and purr like house cats. They also have the best eyesight of any cat.

We saved this cat for last. Do you know what it is? It is a male lion. Male lions are known as the king of the jungle because of their raw power and strength. Lions don't fear other animals. The roar of a male lion can be heard 5 miles away. Lions like to live in groups known as a pride. Male lions have mains and females do not. Female lions gather most of the food and male lions protect the herd and the young cubs, baby lions.

Look there's a hippopotamus, also called a hippo. They are the second largest land animal. They have the largest mouth of any land animal. To stay cool, they spend most of their time in the water. Hippos can hold their breath for up to five minutes underwater. When submerged, their ears and nostrils fold shut to keep water out. They sweat an oily red liquid which helps protect their skin and acts as a sunblock, too! Cool, huh?

There's a rhinoceros, also called a rhino. They are huge and can run as fast as a car, up to 55 miles per hour. They have a long horn on their nose that is made from the same stuff as our fingernails. Rhinos have very poor eyesight. They communicate through honks and sneezes. They snort to warn other animals when they get to close. They love playing in the mud and water to keep cool and keep insects from biting them.

What are those animals with long legs and necks? They are Giraffes. They are the tallest mammal on earth. Their long legs and neck help them to eat leaves from the trees. They like to eat leaves. New-born baby giraffes are taller than most humans and they can stand within 30 minutes. Giraffes live up to 25 years. Giraffes can sleep standing up like a horse. Giraffes are super peaceful animals. They are easy to get along with.

Elephants are the largest land animal. They have huge ears. They can grab stuff with their trunks. Elephants eat all day long. They can't jump like other animals and humans. Elephants communicate with vibrations in the ground. Baby elephants can stand within 20 minutes after birth. Elephants are very smart, they never forget anything. Elephants purr like cats do.

Author Page

Billy Grinslott & Kinsey Marie Books

Copyright, All Rights Reserved

ISBN – 9781965098295

Thanks

www.ingramcontent.com/pod-product-compliance
Lightning Source LLC
Chambersburg PA
CBHW060847270326
41934CB00002B/34